A POCKET POSITIVE
GUIDE TO
DEMENTIA
BRIAN LAWLOR

About the author

 **Brian Lawlor** is Conolly Norman Professor of Old Age Psychiatry at Trinity College Dublin and Consultant Psychiatrist and Director of the Memory Clinic at St. James's Hospital Dublin. He graduated in Medicine from University College Dublin in 1980 and trained initially in general medicine in Ireland and then in psychiatry in the United States at the University of Florida, the National Institutes of Health, Bethesda, Maryland and Mount Sinai Medical Center, New York before returning to Ireland in 1991.

He has been working in the field of dementia care for over 30 years and has published extensively in the area of Alzheimer's disease and dementia. His special interests are in the early detection of Alzheimer's disease, the management of behavioural and psychological symptoms of dementia and in the development of new treatments and interventions in Alzheimer's disease.

Acknowledgement

I would like to acknowledge the encouragement and creative input of Sabina Brennan of the NEIL Programme, TCD who provided valuable advice at an important stage of the book's creation and for the time she spent editing a number of earlier drafts.

I would also like to express my appreciation to Mary and Davis Coakley for their time and effort in proof reading and editing the book.

Finally, and most importantly, I would like to thank the many patients and families who have shaped and framed my experience in caring for people with dementia and helped generate these positive messages that I hope will be of help to a new generation of doctors involved in brain health and dementia care.

Published in 2015 by:
Trinity Brain Health, Trinity College Dublin,
Dublin 2, Ireland

©Copyright Trinity Brain Health

ISBN 978-0-9934806-0-7

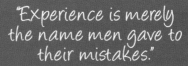

"Experience is merely the name men gave to their mistakes."

Oscar Wilde - The Picture of Dorian Gray

Preface

It can be difficult sometimes to know what to do, what to say and how to help people with dementia and their caregivers.

For this reason, I thought that it might be helpful to share some of the lessons that I have learned over the last 30 years, drawing on my own professional experience in caring for people with dementia.

The aim of the pocket guide is to provide sensible and easy-to understand advice on how best to interact effectively with people with dementia and their families and most importantly how to communicate positively with them. The guide also includes some advice and tips on assessment and on what I have found to be helpful to do or say in difficult circumstances.

When I started to write this dementia guide, I had doctors in mind as the target audience but I think that many of the topics will also be of interest to other health care professionals and to family members of people with dementia.

I hope that these 'bite-sized' pieces of information will help you to interact in ways that are rewarding for both you and for the person with dementia, whether you are the treating doctor, a health care professional or a family member involved in their care.

Table of Contents

1. THE RIGHT ATTITUDE

It is all about the person, not the disease

If you focus on the person and not the disease itself, there is always something that can be done to help the person. The person, your patient, is looking to you for answers, advice and direction. By virtue of the fact that you are a doctor, the patient has already invested great trust in you. You must respond to that trust in a positive way and in the case of a disease like Alzheimer's, always try to instill some hope and create room for positive action following the diagnosis.

No matter what stage of the illness the person is at, you have to try and reach that person when you are communicating. There is always the temptation to talk over the person; you must resist it at all costs

A common complaint from patients and families over the years is that we as doctors do not speak to the person with dementia, that we talk over them and that we explain issues to family members but not to them. It is relatively easy to fall into this trap. Very often, patients with Alzheimer's disease can understand much more than they can express; it is more important to err on the side of communicating directly with the person, even if they have trouble understanding, than to ignore the person and deal only with the family member. As in most situations, depending on the person and the stage of the illness, we have to find a balance but always try to favour the patient in that equation.

Different stages have different treatment approaches

In managing Alzheimer's disease, your approach must take into consideration the stage the person and the family are at in terms of the diagnosis and care journey. The person with the illness may minimise or deny symptoms and their impact early on, as indeed may the family. It is important to try and distinguish this denial from lack of awareness or insight. Be cautious about stripping away denial at the early stage as this may well be an important defence mechanism that the patient needs to keep in place, at least for a period of time. One exception to this rule is where there are risk issues that arise from this denial; in this situation, confrontation will be necessary for safety reasons.

Talk to the person, but always listen to the family

The family is usually but not always correct in providing the history and background. Even when it is difficult to detect changes in cognition, if you have a reliable family member providing a history of cognitive decline, this must be taken seriously. The collateral history is often more sensitive in detecting early changes than objective based performance tests. This is particularly true in individuals who have high educational and occupational attainment. In these instances, while they may perform within a normal range for their age and education, their performance may represent a decline from their previous level of abilities.

The family is usually but not always right when it comes to reporting cognitive decline and memory problems

Sometimes, where there is strong denial in family members, they can under-report symptoms or impairment. Conversely, if a family member is distressed or depressed, they can over-report impairment and symptoms. It is important to consider the family caregiver's perspective and emotional state when taking the history.

Often, the patient with dementia will surprise you with their sense of humour, understanding and appreciation

It is very easy to underestimate a person's abilities when they have dementia. One patient suddenly stopped me when I was conducting the Mini-Mental State Examination (MMSE) and had just asked him to remember the 3 words and said to me 'you know that I'm a cruci-verbalist'. He could see that I was somewhat perplexed and asked me did I know what that was? He then explained that it was someone who does crosswords! When I asked him to spell WORLD backwards, he turned his back to me and spelt 'W-O-R-L-D'! This was a man with an established dementia who was poking fun at me and indicating to me that the MMSE as a test was somewhat demeaning to him.

Do not underestimate the quality of life of a person with dementia

As doctors, we automatically tend to underestimate an individual's quality of life when they have objective and observable illnesses. We often fail to take into consideration the importance of other factors such as their subjective appraisal of their own health which may be different from ours, and their social and psychological health, all of which impacts on their quality of life. This is the reason that it important to consider interventions that can be positive and have an evidence base, and not to take a nihilistic view of the illness, because a small change can often translate into a large beneficial effect for the individual with dementia and for their family caregiver.

You might be surprised how much a word of kindness or encouragement from the doctor can sustain a person and their family in the face of dementia

Over the years I have learned that what we say and how we say it, even when we as doctors may not remember exactly what we said or when we said it, can be extremely important to the person with dementia and to their family. Many times family members have come back to me years later and quoted some words or advice that I had imparted which to me did not appear that important at the time but which sustained the family and the patient and gave them hope.

Caring is what matters

This is a lesson that I learned a little late in my career. I remember sitting down with a family and agonising over the exact cause of a particular dementia, spending a long time going through the exhaustive differential diagnosis and investigations that we had carried out. The patient's daughter, who was also a health care professional, stopped me mid-sentence and said to me 'we know she has dementia, we're here to find out what you can do to help her and to help us'

Caring for or caring about the person with dementia?

Some would argue that you must separate out caring for and caring about your patient with dementia. Caring about the person means you are able to recognise and respond to the person with dementia and not just see and treat their illness, which is good for both the doctor and the patient.

The language and the words you use are important when talking to people with dementia and to their families

How you explain issues and medical concepts and your attitude and approach in doing so is very important. You have to be able to explain technical and medical terms using understandable words and language. I can remember asking a patient and her son if she had ever been incontinent and her son brusquely replied 'doctor, she's never been outside Dublin'. Using complex terminology in explaining a diagnosis is likely to result in miscommunication. Many doctors have difficulty understanding and communicating the difference between Alzheimer's disease and dementia to one another so it is no wonder that the person and family members get confused. I have found that providing information in written form and in language that the person can understand is helpful but challenging as it forces you to translate medical terminology into bite-sized understandable pieces.

While people die of dementia and many more die with dementia, it is not a terminal illness when first diagnosed and a palliative approach is only appropriate in the very late stages

It is wrong to see Alzheimer's disease and other dementias as terminal illnesses that just require a palliative approach. Like all chronic diseases, there is a terminal phase, but this is quite late in the disease process and we must focus on the general interventions and stage specific interventions that can be made that improve quality of life and even stabilise the disease for a period of time. A failing brain due to Alzheimer's disease is not dissimilar to a failing heart due to ischaemic heart disease. Heart failure is not seen as a terminal illness at diagnosis so why should Alzheimer's disease be considered terminal?

2. THE ART OF HISTORY TAKING IN DEMENTIA

There are three things to remember about taking a history where there is cognitive decline: collateral, collateral, collateral

More so than in other medical conditions, the collateral history is of vital importance in the detection and diagnosis of dementia and Alzheimer's disease. The patient may not be able to give an accurate account of the illness because neurodegeneration can affect insight, awareness and memory. In this situation, we must depend on a reliable collateral history in terms of onset, first symptoms, or behaviours and course over time. A key task in obtaining collateral is to establish the impact of the impairment on the ability to function independently, as this determines whether the person meets criteria for dementia.

In talking to people with dementia and in talking to people in general, it is good to find some common ground; where they come from and what their interests and hobbies are can often be a good starting point

It is not a good idea to head straight into direct questions about memory until you connect and are present with the person. A good 'ice-breaker' is to find out where the person is from and what they worked at, as this also provides information on educational and occupational attainment. Sport, the 'soaps', hobbies and interests can also be a good connection and can help the person to relax into the interview and engage in the testing in a more meaningful way.

It is important to know who the most important people are in the patient's life: not only does this help to establish a relationship with the patient but it can also help with planning interventions

A good question to ask the patient or a collateral source is 'who are the people that have most contact with the individual?' This gives a clear view of the level of social connection or isolation of the individual and will be a key factor in any therapeutic plan or intervention that you might wish to put in place.

In unpicking the history of cognitive decline, find out what happened first.....was it memory, was it language, or was it behaviour?

We often see patients when they are at least 1-2 years into their illness and they can have a mix of symptoms that can be confusing in terms of unpicking the underlying cause. In these circumstances, I advise you to go back to what actually happened first and this is where the collateral history is crucial. Did it start as a language problem (possibly indicating primary progressive aphasia [PPA] or was it memory and then language [more likely Alzheimer's disease] or did it start as a behavioural and personality change with problems with judgement and executive function (which would suggest a fronto-temporal lobar dementia).

Just because there is a stressor does not always mean that the cause of the memory complaint is psychological

Some people may present to you with subjective memory complaints and with prominent anxiety and worry because of this. There may even be an identifiable stressor that can account for the anxiety and cognitive complaints. Testing may be normal or not show any evidence of an Alzheimer pattern but despite the findings on assessment, both the patient and the family may have concerns that there is something going on other than anxiety. I have seen a number of cases like this which I originally considered to be anxiety or simply subjective memory complaints which presented again 5-7 years later with Alzheimer's disease. In cases like this, it is best to treat the anxiety and address the underlying cause if possible but still recommend that the person return for repeat assessment if there is evidence of any deterioration.

It is important to understand what patients mean when they say they have a problem with their memory

The words 'memory loss' can be used incorrectly by both the lay public and by doctors. Sometimes a person may be referred with memory loss, but that person turns out to have a problem with forgetting words or forgetting the meaning of words, which points more to a language disorder. Likewise, a person may say that they have a memory problem when it is more an issue with attention and concentration and not memory per se. It is a good idea to ask the person what they mean by 'memory loss' and to give you specific examples.

Making and losing memories

I have found the 'information processing' model of memory to be useful in explaining to students and to patients where and why a person's memory is failing. In this model, memory 'parcels' are first of all placed in short term (or working) memory for immediate use and then encoded (or 'wrapped') before getting stored (or consolidated) in long term memory from which they can be later retrieved. To make a memory, first, you must be able to perceive (hear, see) so that information can get in. Secondly, you must attend and concentrate, otherwise you cannot encode information. This requires a certain level of arousal in order to get the information into 'working (or short term) memory'. Next the information is consolidated and stored. Finally, you need to be able to retrieve the information from storage.

Different diseases can affect the memory system at differing stages; e.g. Alzheimer's disease affects consolidation; depression and anxiety affect encoding; fronto-temporal lobar dementia affects encoding and working memory.

Memory loss means different things to different people

You can often tell from the history what the memory problem is due to and the part of the brain that is affected. Misplacing where you put something or forgetting what you went into the room to get is more due to lapses in attention than to a memory problem. Forgetting how to operate a TV remote or how to use the oven is a procedural memory problem and may reflect problems with frontal lobe functioning rather that memory per se. Repeating stories, asking repeated questions, forgetting appointments, what you have to do or have just done, who visited you, what you had for breakfast or whether you actually had breakfast: these are examples of a primary memory problem. If there is clear evidence of rapid forgetting i.e. the individual forgets information rapidly and completely after a delay, this usually represents a hippocampal problem and these individuals are more likely to have Alzheimer's disease.

There are sensitive indicators from the history that flag when you should be concerned that the person has a significant cognitive problem

If the person has a problem with orientation to place and way finding, or is having problems with managing finances, then I would say that there is a definite problem with their cognition and it must be looked into. Good questions to ask about higher order functioning are managing banking needs, paying bills, driving ability and how successfully would the person negotiate an airport if travelling on their own. This last question, 'the airport question', has very strong face validity in indicating that there is a real underlying problem with memory or cognitive functioning-that is of course if the person uses an airport when travelling!

Balancing the risk and the 'dignity of risk' in dementia

Risk issues to consider in people with dementia include legal, financial and safety. People with dementia are vulnerable and are at risk of making poor financial decisions or being exploited. Execution of an enduring power of attorney is one way to try and protect the patient. Safety issues include not being able to look after themselves, particularly if living alone, wandering at night time, risk to others (e.g. due to aggressive behaviour) and driving. As doctors, we need to raise these risk issues during the interview and address them as part of the management plan. By the same token, there is also a 'dignity of risk'. Risk is part of being human. We must be careful not to be overprotective at all costs and inflexible in our approach to risk. Risk management in dementia should be viewed as an incremental and dynamic process where we always try to achieve the correct balance in the best interest of the person with dementia.

The thorny issue of driving and its assessment

Raising the issue of stopping or retiring from driving because of dementia can often cause great upset and distress to many patients and their families. It can be a thorny but necessary issue to raise at assessment as the safety of the person and others could be at stake. If the person has a diagnosis of dementia, you should take a driving history from the patient and family.

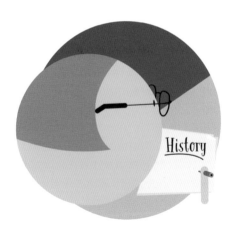

Taking a driving history

Ask is there any way finding difficulty, erratic driving, problems taking right turns, driving too slowly and any 'fender benders'? Difficulty turning right at junctions, poor lane discipline and driving too slowly are the main driving difficulties that families report for people with dementia. If there is evidence of problems with driving on the basis of history, patients should be advised to stop driving and if they refuse, they must take an on road assessment. People with mild Alzheimer's disease may be able to continue to drive if they pass an on road assessment, possibly with restrictions such as only driving locally, avoiding poor weather conditions and not driving at night. On road assessment should be repeated every 6-12 months because dementia is progressive. The doctor should inform patients with dementia or Alzheimer's disease that they are required to tell their insurance company, the Driver Licensing Authority and have an on road assessment.

Fronto-temporal lobar dementia (FTD) does not just present as behavioural and personality change

People who develop FTD can present in a number of ways depending on the location of the pathology in the frontal and temporal lobe areas. If there are prominent behavioural and personality changes, this is the behavioural variant (bvFTD) and the pathology is primarily in the front and middle area of the frontal lobe. However, there are a number of other less common presentations that are worth mentioning. Pathology in the left front part of the frontal lobe area will present with a language problem called progressive non- fluent aphasia (PNFA) where there is difficulty with language expression and articulation. Another type of language presentation is called semantic dementia (SD) where there is a problem with understanding the meaning of words and the pathology is localised to the front part of the temporal lobes. Finally, you can have a motor or

movement disorder presentation as part
of a fronto-temporal lobar dementia; this
can be either an FTD (usually bvFTD) with
motor neurone disease or a Corticobasal
Degeneration or progressive supra-nuclear
palsy (Parkinson's Plus-parkinsonism type
presentation).

The behavioural phenocopy: a puzzle wrapped up in an enigma

I have seen a number of cases where the history is suggestive of a behavioural variant FTD but the person does not progress over time and imaging biomarkers, which should show evidence of neuronal damage in the fronto-temporal areas (either atrophy on CT/MRI or hypometabolism on SPECT/PET) are normal. When someone presents with this type of picture, my advice is to be slow to make the diagnosis of FTD unless you have evidence of executive dysfunction on testing along with some structural or functional neuroimaging confirming neuronal damage to the frontal and temporal lobes. Residual schizophrenia and incompletely treated complex mood disorder or a person with Asperger's experiencing stressful life events could present as a 'behavioural phenocopy' (i.e. looks like but is not) and mimic FTD. Whether some of these enigmatic cases will ultimately turn out to be very slowly progressive FTD cases remains to be seen.

Dementia and Alzheimer's disease are not just memory problems

Despite what you have been taught in medical school, Alzheimer's disease does not always present as a memory problem and a language presentation is not uncommon particularly in younger people. Knowing how to assess language function is important in diagnosing an atypical form of Alzheimer's disease but also in differentiating between some forms of (atypical) Alzheimer's disease and the language presentations of FTD (e.g. semantic dementia [SD]) or progressive non-fluent aphasia (PNFA). The person themselves or their family will say that they have a problem with words or language but at first assessment, it can be hard to distinguish one type of language disorder from another.

The visual variant of Alzheimer's disease, also known as posterior cortical atrophy or Benson's syndrome

Another atypical presentation of Alzheimer's disease is where patients present with 'visuo-spatial problems'- the so called 'posterior' presentation; they may complain of difficulty reading a line of text, judging distances, distinguishing between moving objects and stationary objects, an inability to perceive more than one object at a time, difficulty manoeuvring, identifying, and using tools. The patient often sees the optician before being referred for neurology assessment and there is a delay in diagnosis. A stroke may even be suspected. The underlying pathological cause is usually, but not always, Alzheimer's disease.

The pattern of symptoms and pattern of the presentation usually points to where the pathology is but does not necessarily tell you what the pathology or the underlying diagnosis is

The pattern of symptoms will help to localise where the brain problem is (frontal, temporal, parietal, anterior or posterior) but does not tell you what the pathology is. A problem localising to the hippocampus (i.e. memory) usually means Alzheimer's disease but not always. Behavioural and personality change in a younger person usually point to an FTD but it could be due to a frontal variant of Alzheimer's disease. A semantic language problem usually suggests lobar FTD pathology but can also be due to AD. A motor presentation should make you think of non-AD pathology but Alzheimer's disease may still be found at autopsy. Structural imaging likewise tells you where the damage is but not the cause. This is where molecular imaging (PET amyloid) and CSF biomarkers can provide the answer to what is the underlying pathology. Where we suspect lobar pathology with frontal presentations, we can be proven to be wrong at autopsy or when cerebrospinal fluid (CSF) biomarkers confirm an Alzheimer's disease signature.

The cognitive continuum: from brain health to dementia

In meeting with patients and families to explain the results of the cognitive assessment, I have found it useful to talk about the 3 broad categories across the continuum of cognitive impairment and then to explain where I believe this person currently sits. It is important to emphasise that these are not exact definitions and that people do not move seamlessly from one category of cognitive impairment to the next.

Subjective memory complaints This is where there are subjective complaints but normal testing based on age and education norms.

Mild cognitive impairment This is where there are subjective complaints or there is an informant report or clinician observed decline with neuropsychological test results 1.5 SD below age/education norms and 'essentially normal day to day function'.

Dementia Here, there are subjective and/or informant reports with neuropsychological testing >2SD below age/education norms and loss of function (i.e. disease or illness range).

I AM A
FAMILY DOCTOR
IS THERE A GOOD WAY TO CHECK OUT A
MEMORY
COMPLAINT?

'High flyers'

By 'high flyers' I mean individuals with memory complaints who have a very high pre-morbid IQ, and while they score within the normal range for their age and education, they may be performing lower than predicted by their IQ on neuropsychological tests. These individuals can be difficult to diagnose and may be aware themselves of decline but the testing is not showing the problem because of their high intellectual capacity. However, once you have a baseline, you can repeat testing in 12 months to see if there is any decline and this can help with the diagnosis. This is where biomarkers, either imaging or cerebrospinal fluid (CSF), may be required in the future to help clarify if and when such individuals are developing dementia.

The Mini-Mental State Examination

The MMSE can be a poor test of cognition when given just on its own. Age and education must be considered in interpreting a high or a low score on the MMSE. Be careful not to over interpret a low MMSE score in an older person particularly if they have poor education where the collateral history does not suggest cognitive decline. By the same token, be careful not to be falsely reassured by a high MMSE score, especially in well-educated or younger individuals if they or their family are reporting change in memory or cognition. The usual cut-off for dementia on the MMSE is <24 but with the above health warning! It is important to remember that the MMSE does not test executive or frontal lobe function at all and this is one of its main deficiencies as a screening tool for dementia. I can remember one particular patient with bv FTD who scored 30 out of 30 on MMSE but failed on more specific tests of frontal lobe function and was unable to work due to his dementia.

The Clock Drawing Test

If I could only give one test, I would use the clock drawing test. It is very quick, it can be fun to do, by and large, and it is acceptable to patients. I find that you can get a lot of information not just by looking at what the person has drawn but also by watching the person draw the clock. To do the clock drawing test, you ask the person to draw a clock, put all the numbers in and put the hands reading the time as 10 past 11. The test taps into global cognition, executive and visual spatial functioning. It will often be normal in people with a mild AD but seriously affected in those with dementia with Lewy Bodies (DLB) where visual-spatial function is severely affected. Adding the clock drawing test to the MMSE gives you a little more information and at least gives you some measure of executive functioning.

For executive functioning, the best bedside test is verbal fluency for letters (phonemic) and categories (semantic). You should ask the person to generate as many words as they can, beginning with the letter F and/or names of animals in 60 seconds. The person should get >12 in a minute. A good rule of thumb that I have learned is that people with a frontal type dementia will do more poorly on letter fluency than categories whereas Alzheimer patients will do better on letter fluency than on categories, because semantic (category) fluency is localised to the temporal lobes, which are more affected in AD.

Delayed word recall as a 'hippocampal test'

Because Alzheimer's disease pathology begins in the entorhinal cortex and hippocampus, tests that map onto this brain area are more likely to be sensitive to the detection of Alzheimer's disease at an earlier stage. A good test that I recommend in this regard is the Delayed Word Recall Test (DWR) which is easily administered in the clinic. 10 words on cards are presented; each of the 10 words is shown to the person in sequence; the person has to say the word and put the word into a sentence to encode them and this is repeated X 1. You then use a distractor task e.g. copy pentagons, clock drawing task for 5 minutes. You then get the person first of all to free recall the 10 words. To evaluate recognition memory you then show the person 10 cards each with 4 words, one of the words being a word that they had been shown previously. Scoring <3 on free recall or <10 on recognition memory is within the Alzheimer's disease range and if someone with MCI has these scores, this would point to an Alzheimer's disease signature or prodromal phase of Alzheimer's disease. If someone has a high score on recognition memory on this test, even if they forget things rapidly and have the early stages of Alzheimer's disease, this usually indicates that hints, prompts and aide-memoires would be helpful strategies for this person. We have found that this is very useful and positive information to provide to patients and their families at feedback.

Everyone is 'doing the MoCA'

It is not a dance or a coffee, it's the Montreal Cognitive Assessment which is gaining increasing popularity in clinical practice as a brief assessment tool for cognitive impairment. Stated advantages over the MMSE are that it's better for the detection of MCI and for milder cases of dementia, and indeed, I have found this to be the case. The MoCA is also better from the point of view of testing for frontal-executive function as it includes a Trail Making Test, verbal fluency and an assessment of the ability to abstract. Like the MMSE, it's scored out of 30. The original cut off of <26 for MCI is probably too high and less than 24 is probably more accurate in terms of cut-off for impairment. However, age and education influence performance and I have found that there is a real danger of overestimating the number of individuals with dementia and MCI by virtue of getting a low score. Also, it's important to always include the prompting and cue part of the recall task. If you do not, you may assume that the person has a significant memory problem when in fact they do not. Although it is not scored on the form, I often find that patients score zero out of 5 on recall but when I prompt with category and multiple choice, they can remember the words. If the patient does not benefit from cueing, then they are likely to have a real problem with memory; if they do benefit from cueing, as many people do, a zero score could be due to poor attention, depression and anxiety or vascular causes.

Some helpful hints on assessing language in dementia

If the person presents with prominent language symptoms, the first thing to establish is whether there is evidence of single word comprehension which would indicate a semantic dementia. This can be picked up by asking the person to repeat a word (which they will be able to do) and then to point to the picture of the word (which they will find problematic because they will not be able to identify the object due to the semantic problem) - this is called the repeat and point test. In contrast, the person with PNFA will have difficulty repeating the word but no problem identifying the object in the picture. It is important to distinguish between PNFA and the wording finding/searching of a language presentation of Alzheimer's disease: PNFA speech is hesitant and effortful and the person makes grammatical errors; in Alzheimer's disease, there is a problem finding the words but the person still understands the meaning of words and there is no problem with grammar (referred to as logopenic pattern). In addition to using the repeat and point test, I have found it useful to have the person describe a picture and write down verbatim what they say, almost like a brief transcript, and then examine it for the above characteristics. This should help you distinguish between PNFA, semantic and logopenic AD.

Is it depression or dementia?

Where there are mixed features of depression and memory loss, my experience is that the best approach is to do a work-up for dementia and treat the depression. Once the depression has been treated, I re-assess the level of cognitive impairment. Depression and anxiety can be early associated features of the pre-dementia state and if present, can lower the threshold for the clinical expression of the dementia. When the depression and anxiety are treated, the level of cognitive impairment can improve but dementia could still re-emerge over time if indeed the depression was an indicator of a pre-dementia state.

Mild cognitive impairment: a millstone or a milestone?

Mild cognitive impairment means a degree of cognitive impairment that is not normal but is not dementia i.e. there is essentially normal function. While the term has some clinical utility, exactly what is meant by 'essentially normal function' and how to define 'cognitive impairment but not dementia' remains controversial.

It is crucial from the collateral history to make the best judgement possible regarding whether the cognitive problem is interfering with everyday functioning. In MCI, functioning is 'essentially' normal but of course, when people are retired, the threshold for impairment is much lower. In an early onset case, where a person is still working, the bar defining loss of function will be set much higher.

In terms of assessment, for the individual with mild symptoms and high education who seems to be functioning normally, in my experience, there is little point in doing an MMSE as it is too easy a test: it is far better and more useful to do a MoCA and get an Alzheimer Questionnaire filled in by the next of kin to determine if there is a change in memory compared to before.

Biomarkers as diagnostic tools

Biomarkers are now being used more frequently in academic and research settings to try and clarify the underlying cause of MCI earlier. In other words, can we establish whether the case of MCI is due to AD or some other pathology? The biomarkers that appear to be useful are hippocampal atrophy on MRI or CT (coronal views), a pattern of low CSF Aβ 42/high p-Tau or PET amyloid brain imaging. If you have MCI with a hippocampal amnesia and positive biomarker (temporal lobe atrophy, low Aβ 42/high p-Tau, high T-Tau, positive amyloid imaging) then the underlying pathology is most likely to be AD. However, this information is only likely to be available in very specialist research settings and most of the time, as a doctor, you are basing your assessment of the cause of the underlying MCI on the history, MoCA, DWR and neuroimaging which may or may not provide a (coronal) view of the hippocampus and medial temporal lobe.

How do you monitor response to (drug) treatment?

This can be difficult especially in a condition where it is very hard to show improvement. I have found that a good approach, along with repeating an MMSE or MoCA, is to document functions that remain intact (e.g. money management, driving, way finding, use of telephone etc.) at the first assessment and then to review at each follow-up assessment whether these functions remain intact or not. If they are retained, the person is stable from a functional point of view which is what is hoped for.

Tipping points

It is often the behavioural dimension of dementia rather than the cognitive aspects that create the greatest stress and burden for the caregiver and can tip the caregiver rapidly into a crisis.

In assessing behavioural and psychological symptoms in dementia (BPSD), I have found it useful to conceptualise BPSD as comprising clusters or syndromes: agitation, aggression, affective (depression/anxiety) and psychosis.

As part of the history and assessment of all people with dementia, it is important to ask about the presence of behavioural and psychological symptoms (BPSD). BPSD are common in dementia, have a significant impact on the quality of life of patients and their caregivers but most importantly are a potentially treatable aspect of dementia.

There may be co-occurrence and overlaps but I always try to identify what is the predominant behavioural cluster. Is it agitation, aggression, psychosis, sleep disturbance, depression/anxiety? Your intervention and treatment should be targeted and tailored, based on available evidence base for that cluster.

In my experience, depression as the sole cause of cognitive impairment that results in interference with day to day functioning ('depressive pseudo-dementia') is rare; it is much more common to see co-morbid depression and dementia/cognitive impairment

The patient may not always present with a classical full-blown syndrome of depression. Many cases of depression are not that obvious at interview as the person may not appear pervasively depressed: the history from the family is more informative and should influence whether you treat or not, always keeping in mind the risk/benefit ratio of drug treatment. Anxiety/depression should be managed in the first instance by activation and engagement. Antidepressant medication may be useful in more severe or persistent cases.

Assessing depressed mood in the person with dementia

Ask the person or family about sense of humour and engagement with family or friends or how they feel about the future. Ask the family if the person has made any statements that might indicate hopelessness. In more severe cases where the person is unable to report their subjective experience, the family member can often tell you whether the person is sad, withdrawn, tearful, all of which may indicate the presence of depression

Many cases of depression in dementia are below 'case' level but can still need and respond to intervention: listen to the family

Sometimes I find that there is a mismatch between what I see in the clinic when I talk to the patient and what the family report about the patient's demeanour at home. Members of the family may say that the person is very depressed and withdrawn at home and is tearful and miserable, but the patient presents differently in the clinic. I always encourage engagement and behavioural activation through a day centre as it can be helpful; however, I have often found that this type of patient presentation can show a good response to antidepressant treatment.

Misidentifications can be confusing to caregivers and to doctors

It is always important to enquire about perceptual abnormalities (i.e. delusions, hallucinations) as part of BPSD. A person may be experiencing perceptual abnormalities, and the family or caregiver, while aware that there is something wrong, may not be able to articulate it to the doctor because it is such an unusual experience for them. For example, a person fails to recognise his own image in a mirror, believing it to be someone else and then becomes distressed and possibly develops persecutory beliefs about this 'other person'. This is the so called 'mirror sign' and is a misidentification of self. This can be dealt with by removing or covering mirrors and, if there is secondary delusional elaboration with distress, antipsychotic medication may be of some benefit. Other misidentifications that can occur are misidentifying a spouse or family member, believing that they are imposters;

misidentifying the house as not their own home and wanting to go 'home' to a former residence. It is important to explain to families that these are perceptual abnormalities often with delusional (false and fixed) beliefs that are not amenable to argument. Arguing the case can cause even more distress and may result in risk to the caregiver. I have learned from experience that the best approach is general reassurance and distraction as the misidentifications may not persist.

5. FUNCTION IN DEMENTIA: A FORGOTTEN DIMENSION THAT MUST BE REMEMBERED

Knowing the functional abilities of your patient is vital for care planning

In addition to cognition and behaviour, it is crucial to consider the functional ability of the individual with dementia and to be able to assess it because the level of function often defines the care needs of the patient.

What we mean by instrumental and personal activities of daily living

You should consider both personal activities of daily living (eating, washing, dressing, toileting) and instrumental activities of daily living (money management, driving, cooking, community engagement) in the assessment. People with dementia due to Alzheimer's disease usually lose function in an ordinal and predictable fashion, losing instrumental activities (money management, driving) first and then personal activities (grooming, toileting, bathing, eating). If a function is lost suddenly or is lost out of sequence, you should consider whether there is an infection like a UTI or if a vascular event has occurred. I have learned the hard way that every acute change in behaviour or mental state in an older person, particularly an older person with underlying cognitive impairment, warrants a dip stick in the urine.

Most of the time but not all of the time, what a caregiver reports about function actually maps onto what the person can do

Functional decline over time is what defines dementia but it can be difficult sometimes to be clear if there is a true decline as we rely almost entirely on proxy reporting from a collateral source, usually a family member.

Sometimes you will find that if caregivers are depressed or very much burdened they may over emphasise functional decline in the person; on the other hand caregivers might be in denial and as a result under-report the degree of functional decline.

Correlating cognitive and functional decline: it is not a straight line

MMSE scores can be roughly mapped to level of function in Alzheimer's disease;

Mild dementia 18-26; problems with driving, money management, use of telephone and machinery, keeping appointments, cooking, high order person hygiene e.g. dental hygiene

Moderate dementia 10-17; travelling alone, grooming, dressing, bathing, toileting

Severe dementia <10; feeding, continence, walking, swallowing

When there's a mismatch between function and MMSE score, this may indicate that the dementia is not due to typical Alzheimer's disease. A relatively high MMSE score and poor function suggests that there could be significant frontal involvement which will not be picked up by the MMSE and may indicate a vascular or frontal lobar pathology as a cause of the dementia.

Loss or the preservation of function is often a better way to assess decline or stability in the course of dementia than measuring change in cognitive function

I have found that this is particularly true in trying to determine if a person might be benefiting or getting worse on a medication. A good question to ask is whether the person is still able to carry out the functions now that they were carrying out at the last assessment. If they are, then function is stable and the person would appear to be benefitting from the medication.

6. DELIRIUM: DEMENTIA'S FREQUENT CHAPERONE

When you see an older person in the hospital or community who has cognitive impairment and is referred for assessment of agitation or depression be sure not to miss hyperactive (looks agitated) or hypoactive (looks quiet, subdued) delirium

Ask yourself: was the behavioural change acute in onset and is there fluctuation in level of consciousness or awareness. Then assess attention as this is the key domain affected by delirium.

Be careful not to diagnose depression when in fact the person is quietly delirious i.e. a hypoactive delirium

The person with dementia who is agitated, distressed and anxious may have both a delirium and BPSD.

Always check the urine for infection and consider the possibility of delirium in an older person with acute behavioural change. The other thing to think about is whether the person with dementia could be in pain. Simple analgesia can relieve agitation due to pain very easily.

Delirium is a stress test for dementia

The main risk factors for delirium are increased age and underlying brain disease. If an older person presents with an acute delirium, there is likely to be an underlying cognitive issue and if they do not have a dementia, there is an increased risk of the emergence of cognitive impairment and dementia further down the road.

Preventing delirium can protect brain health and function in people with dementia.

It is important to diagnose and intervene quickly in delirium as it can prevent deterioration in the context of dementia. Always consider a possible infection (urinary or respiratory tract being the most common sources) if there is an acute change in behaviour in someone with dementia.

Testing for delirium

The first question is whether there has been an acute change in mental state. If so, you must go on and determine if there is evidence of a change in attention. You have to focus on attention as this is the domain affected by delirium. A test of sustained attention that you can do at the bedside, in clinic and even in the ICU is the best approach to assessment.

Ask the person to squeeze your hand every time you say the letter 'A' and then spell out HAVEAHEART. If the person cannot follow you or misses the 'A', and has an acute change in mental state with fluctuation in awareness or consciousness, then it is likely that they have a delirium.

I AM A
FAMILY DOCTOR
IS THERE A GOOD WAY TO CHECK OUT A
**MEMORY
COMPLAINT?**

7. DISCLOSING THE
DIAGNOSIS

The right to know, the right not to know

It is important to have an idea in advance of how much the person wants to know. The person has a right to know the diagnosis, but equally has a right to decide that they do not want to know. The default position for the doctor should be to disclose and discuss the diagnosis but sometimes it has to be done in stages.

It is not necessarily a good idea to overwhelm the person with information at the first visit or to 'beat them over the head with insight'- this might not be appropriate and sometimes, denial is there for a reason such as to protect the individual from depression.

What do you do if the person says 'If I'm told it's Alzheimer's disease, I'll kill myself'?

This is a scenario that has happened to me a number of times and which has caused me considerable anxiety as I was then faced with the difficult task of disclosing the diagnosis to that person. It is best to first tease apart the person's fear of the diagnosis and to try and understand why they fear it. Sometimes the fear relates to a misunderstanding of what Alzheimer's disease is and to a lack of appreciation of the different stages of the disease, for instance the fact that most people at the earlier stages have a good quality of life. In disclosing the diagnosis in these circumstances, the availability of family or more formal supports such as social worker input is very important.

'Whatever you do, don't tell him he has Alzheimer's disease, he won't be able to handle it'

Sometimes the family will call you in advance to tell you that you must not tell the person that they have Alzheimer's disease as it will have devastating consequences. It is important that the family knows that you cannot lie to a patient and that you must disclose the appropriate information if requested by the patient; however, it is also important to listen to the family as they may know something about the patient that you do not. In circumstances such as this, I have found that it is a good idea to be guided by the patient to see what and how much they wish to know. Often, there is such a lack of awareness that it is unnecessary and inappropriate to force the information on the patient when in fact it is not requested or when it cannot be appreciated or understood.

Explaining the difference between Alzheimer's disease and dementia

It may be necessary once again to help the person and family to understand the difference between dementia and Alzheimer's disease. Dementia is the description of a combination of cognitive symptoms and behaviours that result in loss of function. It is not a single disease but can be caused by many different diseases. The commonest cause of dementia is Alzheimer's disease and the reason for carrying out the extensive investigations (dementia work-up) is to delineate, as clearly as possible, what is the underlying cause of the dementia so that the correct treatment can be applied.

Take time and take your time in disclosing the diagnosis

You cannot rush the disclosure process. Give yourself and the patient the time to do it right and follow the patient's and family members' cues. In broaching the issue of the diagnosis and the underlying cause of the cognitive disorder, it's important to start with a review of what the patient already understands or thinks is the problem. This quickly gives you an idea of the level of understanding, denial, or insight that the patient might have. Give the information in simple terms and bite -size pieces and after each piece, check that the patient and the family understand the information that you have just imparted

Breaking it down into 'bite-sized' pieces

It is helpful at the outset to summarise the results of all the tests and findings before jumping to your conclusions. This brings the person and family along with you.

At each step of the process it is a good idea to ask the person if they understand the information so far.

Once the results of the blood test, memory tests and scans have confirmed that there is or is not a significant problem and into which of the 4 categories the person fit (normal, Subjective Memory Complaints, Mild Cognitive Impairment or dementia), it is useful to ask again if the person has a sense of what is the cause of the memory problem, it should be broken gently that there are a number of possible causes such as vascular, neurodegenerative such as AD, vitamin deficiencies and then to say what you believe to be the most likely cause is in this case.

After disclosure, the discussion can move to issues such as medication, lifestyle interventions and any safety issue such as driving that may need to be assessed; enduring power of attorney (EPOA) should also be raised at this juncture.

It is important to be positive and emphasise in a realistic and honest way what can be done and not to focus on the negatives.

8. WHAT TO SAY TO THE PERSON WITH DEMENTIA

The fear of developing Alzheimer's Disease

For older people, a diagnosis of Alzheimer's disease or dementia can be devastating and many older people fear it far more than cancer. Behind this fear is the belief that cancer is treatable whereas dementia is not. However, an important message to impart, in a realistic manner, is that while dementia and Alzheimer's disease are not curable, that like any other illness, they are treatable. There are many treatments and interventions for people with dementia; the main limitation can be a negative attitude by the clinician who considers AD to be incurable and therefore not treatable. Furthermore, making a diagnosis and telling the patient the cause of their problems does not change them as a person. It should give them more of a sense of control over what happens now and into the future.

Should I tell my friends I have Alzheimer's disease?

Sometimes patients and families ask whether they should explain to people that they have Alzheimer's disease. My response is: If you had a limp, would you pretend you did not even though it is obvious to everyone? Likewise, if you have a memory problem, it is best to talk about it – people will be more understanding and accommodating than you think. However, patients and their family can make their own choice and one size does not fit all.

How bad will this get and how quickly will it change?

It can be difficult to predict the exact trajectory of the course of Alzheimer's disease in every person. Some individuals show slow progression whereas in others it can be fast. The presence of psychosis, behavioural symptoms and extra-pyramidal features may indicate a more rapid progression but there are still many factors that may accelerate or slow progression that we just do not understand.

I think that it is important to advise patients to stay in the moment, telling them not to look back, and not to look too far forward when dealing with the diagnosis and the illness.

Being positive and encouraging can be hugely important to the person and the family. I advocate advising them that exercise, good diet and the management of any associated vascular risks may help slow transition and is good medicine anyway.

Practical advice on memory

There are some simple tips that you can pass on to your patients. You could give them a tip-sheet which includes the following advice: write things own, stick to a schedule and routine as much as possible but remain active and social engaged.
We strongly recommend regular physical exercise aerobic exercise (walking at a pace that causes one to perspire or sweat a little so that the heart beat goes up) 3 times per week may help to keep the person sharper and slow decline in people with dementia due to Alzheimer's disease.

Taking a holistic approach to your patient's brain health even in the context of having dementia

Many factors can either increase or decrease the threshold for the expression of your patient's symptoms i.e. memory or other cognitive difficulties. For example, increasing age, some genetic risk factors such as apolipoprotein E (APOE), stress, depression , anxiety, change in environment, medical conditions (influenza, heart failure infection, high or low blood pressure) could all increase your patient's cognitive difficulties. Some of these factors are not avoidable or modifiable e.g. age and genetic causes. However, others are modifiable or treatable. It makes sense to advise your patient to manage what they can in the most adaptive way possible. Working with the patient and the family, you can ensure that intercurrent illnesses are treated promptly so as not to lose any cognitive ground. This approach optimises the opportunity to stabilise your patient's cognitive difficulties as much as possible in the face of the dementia.

9. PASSING ON GOOD ADVICE TO CAREGIVERS AND FAMILY

Information and knowledge are the best way to tackle the fear

I have learnt that you cannot provide too much information about dementia to the caregiver but you are often restricted by time. It is useful to have written information available in the office and contact phone numbers and addresses for the local services. It is a good idea to try to map out the patient and caregivers' needs with them and then try match them up with the resources that are available e.g. family, friends, formal services (meals on wheels, nurse contact, day care, respite care, in-home respite).

As a caregiver you must ensure that you get 'time for yourself'

The best piece of advice that you can give to caregivers is that they need time for themselves. If the caregivers do not look after themselves, the person with dementia will also suffer and the caregiver will not be able to continue to care. Getting a good night's sleep is vital. An effective care package will ensure that caregivers get that time for themselves. You should talk to carers about respite for themselves on a daily, weekly, monthly and annual basis. For example, on a daily basis they should try and get half an hour to themselves to have a bath and get some head space; on a weekly basis they should try to get a couple of hours or an afternoon just for themselves to meet friends or go for a walk; on a monthly basis they should try to get a day for themselves for some 'me' time; and on an annual basis they should try to take a week or two for themselves to properly recharge their batteries.

Rational versus emotional reactions in the caregiving role

Another piece of advice for caregivers that I have sometimes used to good effect is to try and react with their head and not with their heart. While dementia will accentuate pre-morbid traits, the person with dementia is not being difficult or doing it on purpose; it is the dementia that is the problem and it is always best to see it that way.

Boosting the caregiver's self-efficacy can help the caregiver deal more effectively with issues

Self-efficacy is about feeling more confident in one's ability to get something done. In terms of caregiving in dementia, a key component of self-efficacy is knowledge and information about the problems of caregiving and how to solve them for the caregiver. It is important to understand where the gaps are in the care system and how they might be filled.

As a doctor, you can improve the self-efficacy of caregivers by advising them to write down their plan on how to deal with certain issues that are troubling them in the caregiving role - this gives them more of a sense of control over what's happening.

It is important that all family members contribute to the care network if possible and rotas can be really worthwhile. This decreases the emergence of family arguments around the provision of care. Sometimes it needs the doctor to call family members in and ask them to sign up to a shared rota; otherwise one individual caregiver could buckle under the pressure if faced with all of the caring.

Getting and accepting help in the home

Sometimes caregivers are reluctant to apply for support services for a number of reasons, partly because of their own denial or lack of acceptance of the problem. Often, it has more to do with the fact that the person with dementia refuses to either try day care or to accept help in the home and the caregiver quite understandably does not want to upset the person. The person with dementia is often very fearful of losing or giving up their autonomy by becoming dependent on outside 'formal' services and refuses the inputs. In these circumstances I explain that sometimes we have to give up some autonomy to maintain our independence or stay well. In this situation, by accepting some help, the person actually can maintain autonomy for longer in his or her own home. Another argument that I often make is that the supports are going to help both the caregiver, who may be also be frail, and the person with dementia; sometimes this argument makes it more acceptable to accept support. Finally, it is important to emphasise the nature of the stress of caregiving and the importance for the caregivers, if they are to continue to care, to get some time for themselves.

Travelling with dementia

Families will often ask the doctor if they should they take the person with dementia on holidays. Going on holidays can be problematic at the middle and later stages of the illness. Routine and structure help support cognitive functioning. When a person is in unfamiliar surroundings and is outside their 'cognitive comfort zone' coping can become more challenging. International travel with jet lag and travelling to other cities could increase the chances of becoming acutely confused and should be avoided where the person is already finding it challenging to cope in unfamiliar surroundings. I have found that there are no exact answers here: It is easier to support travel within the country rather than international travel because the risks are less. I generally suggest that they try a weekend away within the country before travelling abroad to see how the person manages in unfamiliar surroundings. If the family decides to travel, I recommend that there is plenty of support and family to help. It is also a good idea to check that they are insured from the travel point of view should any deterioration occur when travelling abroad. When travelling by air, check with airlines or the airport authorities about what assistance they give to people with disabilities.

When should you think of a nursing home?

Families often ask the doctor when the right time for someone to go into a nursing home is. This question frequently engenders guilt and upset in the caregiver and needs to be talked through. At a certain time point, a nursing home might be necessary and the right move for the person with dementia and the caregiver. The tipping point varies from person to person so it is hard to be dogmatic about when the right time is for each caregiver or person with dementia. In my experience, incontinence can be the tipping point for some, aggression and sleep disturbance for others and misidentification and failure to recognise the caregiver for others. However, it is a very individual decision in all cases.

'Promise me you'll never put me in a nursing home'

This is a common scenario when a caregiver is confronted by the dilemma whereby the caregiver is unable to manage the patient in the patient's own home or in the caregiver's home. In this situation, it is important to acknowledge the previous wishes of the individual and the caregiver's guilt as well as the current reality which make home care untenable. In life, we often make decisions that we turn around at a later date, informed by changing circumstances or life experiences. The crucial question is whether the patient will receive a safer and better quality of care appropriate to their needs in a nursing home than can be provided at home. When the answer to this question is that the nursing home offers the best care option, we must support the caregiver in making this decision.

10. MANAGEMENT & MANAGING EXPECTATION

Medication for memory, what to expect and what not to expect

There is no treatment that can delay onset or slow disease progression for Alzheimer's disease at the moment. There are two classes of medication that can be used to treat the cognitive symptoms of Alzheimer's disease; cholinesterase inhibitors for mild to moderate disease and memantine for moderate to severe disease. While these medications have been shown to have benefit in terms of cognition and to a lesser extent function, their effects are modest and at best we can expect that there will be a stabilisation of the person's condition for a period of 6-9 months. These are symptomatic treatments and do not affect the natural history of the condition which still progresses. I generally tell the person and the family that they are unlikely to see a significant improvement in memory or function on the treatment but what we are looking for is a preservation of functional abilities over a longer period of time on the medication as compared to being on no treatment. We always use these medications in concert with advice on maintaining social connection, cognitive stimulation and physical exercise and addressing any vascular risk factors (e.g. hypertension, hypercholesterolemia, poor diabetes control).

Side effects of cholinesterase inhibitors can be a nightmare

The main side effect of cholinesterase inhibitors is nausea and GI upset which are often dose related and which improves over time or with dose reduction. A potentially more serious but less common side effect of cholinesterase inhibitors is their effect on heart rhythm. I would recommend a baseline ECG before starting cholinesterase inhibitors; sometimes patients are on β blockers or other agents that slow the heart rate and the addition of a cholinesterase inhibitor in individuals with conduction block could precipitate heart block or lead to syncope. Another side effect of cholinesterase inhibitors can be increased dreaming and nightmares. Nightmares in an individual with cognitive impairment can be misconstrued as hallucinations as the person may have difficulty appreciating and remembering the experience as one that occurred as part of sleep or part of waking. Dose reduction or discontinuation of the medication usually deals with the problem.

Use of antipsychotics in dementia and Alzheimer's disease

From the medical perspective there are many negatives to the use of antipsychotics in dementia, in particular the increased risk of death and stroke-like events. Psychosis in dementia is not the same as in functional psychiatric illnesses. Some psychotic syndromes in dementia are related to cognitive or perceptual problems and do not necessarily respond well to antipsychotic treatments e.g. delusional misidentifications. Because of the higher risk to benefit ratio, the use of antipsychotics must be reserved for severe agitation or aggression and psychosis where there is risk to self and/or others. However, I still believe that judicious use of antipsychotics for the right indication, in selected patients, can be immensely helpful but must be carefully monitored at all times.

When you start an antipsychotic in dementia, always think about when you might stop it

In general, a 4-12 week trial of antipsychotic is what is recommended for severe agitation or aggression when there is risk to self and others; you should always look at a trial taper at that point. If the behaviour worsens with dose reduction or discontinuation, then you will have to consider longer term treatment and monitor on an ongoing basis for treatment emergent side effects. It is important to inform the patient, where possible, of the risk/benefit ratio of antipsychotic treatment and to also make families and caregivers aware of it.

What to look for in terms of side effects of antipsychotics

People with dementia who are treated with antipsychotics (or other psychotropics) will develop side effects more quickly and these side effects will be potentially more serious compared to people without dementia. Extrapyramidal side effects can emerge within days and impact on gait and swallowing ability so we advise to start very low, go slow and monitor weekly or biweekly at the beginning. Side effects in people with dementia can often present in a non-specific manner because the person is not able to articulate the nature of the side effect that they are experiencing , e.g. ' slowed down', 'not himself', 'tired', 'more confused'. For example, the development of a chest infection soon after treatment with an antipsychotic could be related to an impact on swallowing and aspiration into the lungs. Collateral from family is vital in order to pick up on early side effects so that medication doses can be adjusted or the drug can be stopped.

Your first line prescription for agitation at home, in respite or in the nursing home should not be a drug

Firstly, it is important to try to understand the context, the person, the environment and the relationship between the person and their caregiver when offering advice on the management of agitated behaviour. I use the following series of questions as a checklist as part of the assessment:

Is there any evidence of infection, pain or did the person receive any new medications?

Has anything changed recently for the person? Are there any new stressors in his or her life or for the family such as illness, bereavements?

What is the level of understanding that the person has and how does their dementia affect them in terms of memory, language and function?

How stressed and burdened is the caregiver and what supports and resources are available to them?

This allows you to build up a profile of the person, the caregiver and the care environment that provides management options and a care plan other than simply prescribing medications. Medication should be reserved for behavioural and psychological symptoms that are severe, pose a risk to themselves or others and do not respond to behavioural interventions.

What to do when agitation does not respond to non-drug approaches

For non-specific agitation and sleep-wake cycle disturbance that does not respond to behavioural intervention, in my experience, trazodone can be helpful and a safer first line alternative to antipsychotics. Trazodone has anti-anxiety properties and improves slow wave sleep.

Adjusting to respite and a nursing home-managing the move

Moving to a nursing home permanently or for respite can be a traumatic and stressful event for the person and is likely to result in increased distress and agitation for many individuals. How the transition is dealt with can be crucial to its success. Providing familiar items such as photographs, ensuring that staff have autobiographical information on the person and know what their preferences are can support a smooth transition. For example, a staff member going through photographs of grandchildren with the person and talking about their former occupation or career can be calming, reassuring and distract the person from the desire to go home. Listening to familiar music that the person likes and talking with them can also help the person settle in. Time is of the essence and you have to dedicate staff time to make it work.

Notes

Notes

Notes

Notes

Notes

Notes

Notes